Two Boxe

The *Oxford Progressive English Reader*s series provides a wide range of reading for learners of English.

Each book in the series has been written to follow the strict guidelines of a syllabus, wordlist and structure list. The texts are graded according to these guidelines; Grade 1 at a 1,400 word level, Grade 2 at a 2,100 word level, Grade 3 at a 3,100 word level, Grade 4 at a 3,700 word level and Grade 5 at a 5,000 word level.

The latest methods of text analysis, using specially designed software, ensure that readability is carefully controlled at every level. Any new words which are vital to the mood and style of the story are explained within the text, and reoccur throughout for maximum reinforcement. New language items are also clarified by attractive illustrations.

Each book has a short section containing carefully graded exercises and controlled activities, which test both global and specific understanding.

# Two Boxes of Gold
## and Other Stories

**Charles Dickens**

1992
Hong Kong
**Oxford University Press**
Oxford Singapore Tokyo

Oxford University Press

Oxford   New York   Toronto
Petaling Jaya   Singapore   Hong Kong   Tokyo
Delhi   Bombay   Calcutta   Madras   Karachi
Nairobi   Dar es Salaam   Cape Town
Melbourne   Auckland

and associated companies in
Berlin   Ibadan

Illustrated by K.Y. Chan

Syllabus designer: David Foulds

Text processing and analysis by Luxfield Consultants Ltd.


ISBN 0 19 585396 2

Printed in Hong Kong
Published by Oxford University Press
18/F Warwick House, Tong Chong Street,
Quarry Bay, Hong Kong

# CONTENTS

# 1

# Two Boxes of Gold

## The telegram

My name is Herbert Blamyre. I am the Assistant Manager at a bank in Lombard Street, and I live with my wife, Minnie, in a little house in London.

We had only been married for a month, and had just returned from a holiday in Ireland, when my adventures began. I had four more days of holiday left, and Minnie and I were sitting in the garden, when the maid came out with a telegram.

The telegram was from the bank's Manager, Mr Schwarzmoor. It said, 'We want you to go to Italy at once on important business. Please hurry. Be at the office at six-thirty. You must take a train from London Bridge by nine-fifteen, and catch the Dover-to-Calais night boat.'

'Herbert, dear, you won't go, you mustn't go!' said Minnie. 'Please, don't go!'

'I must, my dear,' I said. 'The bank has no one to send but me. My partners need me to go. I shall not be gone for long. I must start in ten minutes.'

Mr Schwarzmoor met me when I reached the bank.

'I hope your wife is well,' he said. 'I am sorry to have to ask you to miss some of your holiday, but there was nothing I could do about it. We need you to take some gold to Naples, in Italy. Here it is,' and he pointed to two large chests. 'These boxes are made of iron, but we have covered them with leather, so that they look like ordinary boxes. They are fastened with special combination locks, and they contain a quarter of a million pounds in gold. You must take the money to

Pagliavicini and Rossi, number 172 Toledo, Naples.
The King of Naples expects that there will be
a war, and he needs
the money to buy
5   guns. The names
that open the locks
are "Masinisa", for
the one with
the white star
10  on the lid, and
"Cotopaxo" for
the one with the
black star.'
     I looked at the
15  locks. Each had eight
sets of the letters of the
alphabet on it. You could move the letters around to
make the words, and then the lock would open.
     'Be sure that you do not forget these two words,'
20  Mr Schwarzmoor continued. 'You must open the boxes
when you get to Lyons to make sure all is well. Talk
to no one. Do not make any friends on the way.'
     'I shall pretend to be a travelling salesman,' I said.
     'Please be careful, Blamyre. You are going on a
25  dangerous journey. Do you have a gun?'
     I opened my coat, and showed him my special belt
with a gun in it.
     'Good,' said Mr Schwarzmoor. 'I hope you do not
need to use it. You will stop in Paris tomorrow. I have
30  some letters for you to give to our business friends,
Lefebre and Desjeans, and you will then go on to
Marseilles by the night train. You catch the boat from
Marseilles to Naples on Friday. We will send you a
telegram at Marseilles. Are the letters for Paris ready,
35  Mr Hargrave?'

'Yes, sir, nearly ready. Mr Wilkins is working on them now.'

## On the boat from Dover

I reached Dover before midnight, and at once got four porters to carry my chests down the stone steps leading to the Calais boat. The first was taken safely on to the boat, but while the second was being carried down, one of the men slipped. He would have fallen into the water, but he was caught by a large man who, with his wife, was just in front of me.

'Steady, my man,' he said. 'Why, what have you got there?'

'Don't know, sir,' replied the porter. 'I only know it's heavy enough to break a man's back.'

'These steps cause a lot of trouble when bringing down heavy goods,' said a voice behind me. 'I see, from your luggage, that we may be in the same business.'

I looked round as we stepped on board. The man who had spoken to me was tall and thin. He had a rather large nose, and a long thin face.

I replied that I was a travelling salesman, and that I thought we might be going to have a rough journey across to France.

'Yes, the weather is very bad tonight,' he said. 'I advise you to find your cabin at once. The boat, I see, is very crowded.'

I went straight to my cabin, and lay down for an hour. At the end of that time I got up and went into the passenger lounge. At one of the small tables sat six of the passengers, among them the two I had already met. They were talking and drinking, and I went over to join them. The large man introduced himself as Major Baxter. He had been in India for many years. The other said his name was Levison.

'It's getting very hot down here,' said the Major. 'Why don't we three go up on deck and get some fresh air? Julia, my wife, is always ill on these boats. She went straight to our cabin, and we won't see her again until
5  we arrive in France.'

When we got on deck, I saw, to my great surprise, four other cases exactly like mine. I could hardly believe my eyes, but there they were, leather covers, combination locks and everything else.

10  'Those are mine, sir,' said Mr Levison. 'I am working as a travelling salesman for the House of Mackintosh. Those cases contain the best waterproof overcoats in the world. We have used these cases for many years. But I know that many people have cases that look
15  like these, and this sometimes leads to mistakes. However, I would think your goods are much heavier than mine. What do you carry? Gas pipes, railway chairs, knives, or something else made of metal?'

I did not reply.

20  'Sir, I think you will do very well in your work,' said Levison. 'Trade secrets should not be discussed in public. Don't you think so, Major?'

'You're quite right, sir,' replied the Major. 'One cannot be too careful.'

25  'There's the Calais light,' cried someone at that moment, and soon after that we were getting ready to leave the boat.

I thought no more about my travelling companions. We parted at Paris. I went my way and they went their
30  way. The Major and his wife were going to stay with some friends who lived in Dromont, near Lyons. From there he would go to Marseilles, then on to Alexandria, in Egypt. Mr Levison was also going to Marseilles, like myself and the Major, but not by my train. He had too
35  much to do in Paris first.

## On the train

I had delivered my letters in Paris and was on my way back to my hotel with Mr Lefebre, a great friend of mine. It was about six o'clock and we were crossing the road, when a carriage passed us. In it was 5 Mr Levison, with his four boxes at his side. I waved to him, but he did not seem to notice me. In the same street we saw the Major and his wife, on their way to the railway station.

At midnight, I was standing at the station watching my luggage being put on to the train. A carriage drew up and an Englishman got out. It was Levison, but I saw no more of him, for the crowd just then pushed me forward. 15

I found a seat in a compartment with only two other people in it. They were already asleep and I could not see their faces. Once the train had started, I fell asleep, too, and dreamed of my dear wife, and our home. Then I began to worry, for I dreamed I had forgotten the 20 words which would open the combination locks. I tried hard to remember, but it was no good. Then I was in the bank at number 172 Toledo, Naples, being ordered to give the words, or be put to death by soldiers. I must give the words, or tell where I had hidden the boxes, for I seemed to have hidden them for some reason. The soldiers pointed their guns. I cried out, 'Please God, show me the words,' and then I woke up.

'Dromont, Dromont. Ten minutes to Dromont,' called the guard.

At Dromont I got off the train and went to the station restaurant for a cup of coffee. Suddenly three or four noisy young Englishmen came hurrying in, with a quieter, older man. It was Levison again. They led him along, and called for champagne.

'Yes, yes,' the leader said. 'You must have some, too, Levison. We have won three games, you know. You will be able to get your money back before we arrive in Lyons.'

Levison talked cheerfully about the last game of cards and drank the champagne. In a few minutes the young men had drunk theirs, and gone out to smoke. In another moment Levison saw me sitting there.

'Well, I am glad to see you,' he said. 'My dear sir, you must have some champagne with me.' He called to the waiter, 'Another bottle of champagne, if you please.' Then, turning to me he said, 'I hope to join you before we get to Lyons. Those others are too noisy for me. Besides, I do not want to lose too much money.'

The waiter brought the bottle of champagne. Levison took the bottle at once.

'No,' he said to the waiter, 'I never allow anyone to open wine for me.'

He turned his back on me to remove the wire. He had taken it off, opened the bottle, and was filling my glass, when a man ran up to shake hands with me. He was in such a hurry that he knocked into Mr Levison and the bottle of champagne was broken.

It was the Major, hot, as usual, and very eager to talk to us.

'Oh, I am so sorry. Let me order another bottle. How are you gentlemen? How lucky to meet you again. I've put Julia on the train, and now she's asleep, with the luggage. More champagne please! What's "bottle" in French? Such an annoying thing has happened, you know. We got here this afternoon and found that those friends of Julia's have gone away on holiday. They'd forgotten we were coming. Very bad, very bad. So, now we're going to Marseilles, too.'

Levison looked rather angry. 'I shall not see you for a while,' he said. 'I must find those young men, and see if I can win back some of my money. Goodbye, Major Baxter, goodbye Mr Blamyre.'

The bell rang for us to return to the train.

## A surprise stop

The Major and his wife came and sat in my compartment. They were a very pleasant couple. The Major was
full of stories about his days in India.

5      Soon the train stopped at Charmont, and Levison
came in.

'If you and the Major and Mrs Baxter would care for
a game of cards,' he said to us, 'then I'm willing to play.'

We agreed. We cut for partners. Mrs Baxter and I
10  against the Major and Levison. We won nearly every
game. Levison played too carefully, and the Major
talked and forgot which cards had been played.

Still, it helped to pass the time. When we had played
for long enough we began to talk. Levison started to
15  tell us about his business.

'For years the companies that make waterproof coats
have been searching for something,' he said. 'It is, how
to let the heat from the body escape from the coat,
without letting the rain in. Now I know how to do it.
20  When I get back to London, I shall offer this secret to
the Mackintosh company for ten thousand pounds. If
they refuse the offer, I shall at once open a shop in
Paris. I shall call the new material Magentosh, and make
a lot of money out of it.'

25      'Very clever,' said the Major.

Mr Levison then turned the conversation to the
subject of combination locks.

'I always use combination locks myself,' he said. 'My
two words are "Tortelli" and "Papagayo". Who would
30  guess them? It would take a very clever thief several
hours to work out even one. Do you find the
combination lock safe, sir?' he asked, turning to me.

I replied that I did, and asked what time our train
was due at Lyons.

'We are due at Lyons at 4.30,' said the Major. 'It is now five to four. I don't know why, but I have a feeling that something will happen before we get there. I am always unlucky when travelling. How fast we seem to be going! See how this railway carriage rocks. I am sure we shall have a breakdown before we get to Marseilles.'

I began to feel afraid, but did not show it. Could the Major be planning to do something against me?

'Nonsense, Major, be quiet. You always spoil a journey by worrying about things you can do nothing about,' said his wife.

Then Levison began to talk about his early life. He had been working for a place that made scarves. He talked on and on.

Then the train slowed down, moved on, slowed down again and stopped.

The Major put his head out of the window, and shouted to a passing guard.

'Where are we?'

'This is Fort Rouge, sir. Twenty miles from Lyons.'

'Is anything the matter?'

An English voice answered from the next window.

'A wheel of the luggage van has broken, they tell us. We shall have to wait two hours, take all the luggage off and put it in another van.'

'Good Heavens,' I cried.

Levison put his head out of the window. 'It's true,' he said, drawing it in again. 'Two hours' delay at least, the man says. It's very annoying, but these things happen. We'll have some coffee and play another game of cards. We can each look at our own luggage, or, if Mr Blamyre will go and order supper, I will see to it all. But goodness me, what is that shining out there by the station lamps? Hey, you sir, guard, what is happening at the station?'

'Those are soldiers, sir,' replied the guard. 'They happened to be at the station on their way to Chalons. The station-master has sent them to watch the luggage van, and to see that the luggage is put into the other van safely. No passenger is to go near it, because there are special government stores in the train.'

Levison spat on the ground, and said something under his breath. I supposed he was angry with the French railways.

'I say, sir,' said the Major, 'have you ever seen such large carts?' and he pointed out of the window. I looked and saw two country carts, each with four strong horses, that were standing, empty, under some trees close to the station.

Levison and I tried to get near our luggage, but the soldiers refused to let us get too close. I watched my chests lifted into the new luggage van. I saw no sign of government stores, and I told the Major so.

'Oh, they're clever,' he replied, 'very clever. It may be the empress's jewels, perhaps, in a very small case which looks like ordinary luggage.'

Just then there was a loud, high whistle, as if a signal had been given. The two empty carts moved off quickly and were soon out of sight.

## Marseilles at last

Three hours later we reached Lyons and changed trains for Marseilles.

'I shall have a sleep, gentlemen,' said the Major. 'I suppose the next thing will be this train breaking down.'

'Major, do please be quiet,' said his wife.

I fell asleep at last, but again my dreams were bad. I imagined I was in a city where there were narrow, dark streets. I felt that I was being watched. Four men on horses came riding down the street. They were waving swords, and were coming towards me. I dreamed I had only one hope of safety, and that was to repeat the words of my combination locks. Already the horses were on top of me. I cried out with great difficulty, 'Cotopaxo, Cotopaxo.' A rough shake woke me. It was the Major.

'You're talking in your sleep,' he said. 'Why do you talk in your sleep? It's a dangerous habit.'

'What was I talking about?' I asked.

'Some foreign nonsense,' replied the Major.

'Greek, I think,' said Levison, 'but I can't be sure.'

We reached Marseilles. I was so happy to see the rows of white houses and the fruit trees. I should feel safer when I was on the ship, and my treasure with me. I had noticed that on that long journey from Lyons I had been watched. I had never fallen asleep without waking to find either the Major, or his wife, or Levison looking at me.

We agreed to keep together, and stood by our luggage trying to decide what to do.

'The boat will be the next thing to fail,' said the Major.

And it was. There had been an accident with the engine, and it would not leave until half an hour after midnight.

'Where shall we go?' I asked. 'Our journey seems very unlucky so far. Let's have dinner together. I must send a message first, but then I'm free until half past eleven.'

'I will take you to a small, but very good hotel down by the harbour,' said Levison. 'The Foreigners' Hotel.'

'That's not a very good place,' said the Major, who knew it well.

'Sir,' said Mr Levison, 'there is a new manager there now, or I would not have suggested it to you.'

'I'm sorry,' said the Major, 'I did not know that.'

We entered the hotel, and found it was rather bare and not too clean.

There were only two large rooms left.

'Mr Blamyre and I will just take one,' said Levison, quickly. 'He is going on the boat tonight, so he will not be sleeping here. His luggage can be put in my room, and he can take the room key, in case he comes in first.'

'Now we are all right,' said the Major. 'So far, so good.'

When I got to the telegraph office, I found a telegram waiting for me from London. To my surprise and horror it contained only these words:

*'You are in great danger. Do not wait a moment on shore. There is a plot against you. Go to the police and ask for a guard.'*

It must be the Major. I was in his hands. That friendly manner of his was all a trick. Even now he might be carrying off the chests. I sent a message back:

*'Safe at Marseilles. All right up to now.'*

I ran back to the hotel, which was in a dirty street by the harbour. As I turned the corner, a man came out of a doorway and took my arm. It was one of the men from the hotel. He said in French, 'Quick, quick, sir. Major Baxter wants to see you at once in the dining-room. There is no time to lose.'

## To catch a thief

I ran to the hotel, and hurried into the dining-room. There was the Major, walking up and down in great excitement. His wife was looking out of the window. The Major ran up and took my hand.

'I am a police officer, and my name is Arnott,' he said. 'That man Levison is a well-known thief. He is, at this moment, opening one of your chests. You must help me to catch him. I knew what he was going to do, but I wanted to catch him in the act. Have you got a gun, Mr Blamyre, in case he puts up a fight? I have a strong stick here.'

'I have left my gun in the bedroom,' I said.

'That's bad. Never mind, he may not think of it. You must rush at the door at the same moment as I do. These foreign locks are never any good. It's room number fifteen. Quietly now.'

We came to the door. We listened a moment. We could hear Levison laughing over the word he had heard me say in my sleep. 'Cotopaxo, ha, ha.'

The Major gave the word and we both rushed at the door. It shook, broke and opened. Levison, with my gun in his hand, stood over the open box, ankle deep in gold. He had already filled a huge belt that was round his waist, and a bag that hung at his side. Another bag, half full, lay at his feet. He did not say one word. There were ropes at the window, as if he had been lowering, or preparing to lower, bags into the side street. He gave a whistle, and some vehicle could be heard driving away fast.

'Give yourself up. I know you,' cried the Major. 'Give up, I've got you now.'

Levison's only reply was to fire the gun. Luckily for us, nothing happened. I had forgotten to load it.

Levison threw it at the Major in anger, quickly opened the window and jumped out.

I ran out of the hotel after him, shouting for help. Arnott stayed to guard the money.

A moment more and a wild crowd of soldiers, sailors and other men were following Levison. In the half-dark, (the lamps were just being lit) we raced after him. Many people tried to hit him, hundreds of hands stretched out to catch him. He got away from one, knocked another down and jumped over a third. We had almost caught him, when suddenly his foot caught on something and he fell head-first into the harbour. There was a shout as he splashed and disappeared into the dark water. I ran down the nearest steps and waited while the police took a boat. A grey-haired policeman took me into the boat with them, and they began to drag the harbour with chains for the body.

'They are clever, these old thieves,' said the policeman. 'I remember this man. I knew his face in a moment. He has dived under the ships and got into some boat and hidden himself. You'll never see him again.'

'Yes we shall, for here he is,' cried a second, bending down and lifting a body out of the water by the hair.

'Oh, he was not so clever, I think,' said a man from a boat behind us. It was Arnott. Then he said to me, 'I just came to see how you were getting on, sir. Don't worry about the money. Julia's watching it. He nearly

had you, Mr Blamyre.
He'd have cut your throat
while you were asleep, rather
than miss that money. But I was on
his track. He didn't know me. I often said he would be   5
caught some day. Well, his name is off the books now.
Come, my friends, bring that body to land. We must get
the gold he has in his waist belt. It at least did one
good thing while he had it. It sent him to the bottom
of the harbour.'   10

Arnott told me everything when we returned to the hotel. On the night I had started my journey, he had received orders from the bank's London head office to follow me, and watch Levison. He had not had time to
5  tell my Manager, Mr Schwarzmoor, about this. The driver of our train had been paid by Levison to make the train break down at Fort Rouge, where Levison's men were waiting with the carts. They planned to carry off the luggage in the darkness. This plan failed,
10  because Arnott had sent a message from Paris for soldiers to be sent to the station. Levison had put something in the champagne, too, but Arnott had spilt it. Levison, defeated the first time, had tried other ways. My unlucky talk in my sleep had given him the word
15  for opening one of the chests. The breakdown of the boat, which was quite accidental (as far as we could tell) gave him his last chance.

That night, thanks to Arnott, I left Marseilles with not one single piece of gold lost. The rest of my journey
20  was good. Our bank has done well ever since, and so have Minnie and I.

# GEORGE AND GEOFFREY

## Marriage plans

Cumner is a very pretty village in England. It has one short street of small houses, a police station, a post office and an old inn. Facing you, as you enter the street, is the lovely old church. There is a very large area of grass, called the Common, which has houses on three sides of it. There is a butcher's shop, the big house belonging to Mr Malcolmson, and a small house where Simon Eade, who works for Mr Malcolmson, lives with his wife and son. And there is Mr Gibbs's house, behind a high brick wall.

George Eade, the son of Simon Eade, was a good-looking young man of twenty-six. Like his father, he worked for Mr Malcolmson. He was honest, and a good worker. However, he did not make friends easily, and had a very bad temper at times.

Mrs Eade loved her son very much. She was, therefore, rather jealous when she found out that George was in love with a girl named Susan Archer. The young couple had met when Susan came to Cumner to stay with some friends there. Mrs Eade did not like the girl.

Susan was the daughter of a farmer. Her parents had a large farm, and they did not want their daughter to marry George. They thought that she was much too good for the son of one of Mr Malcolmson's workers.

George had never cared for a woman before, and he fell very much in love with Susan. Susan loved him, too, and they promised to marry as soon as they could.

## Geoffrey Gibbs

At this time there was another man who was interested in Susan, and wanted to make her his wife. His name was Geoffrey Gibbs. He had been left a house and a
5 lot of money by a relation who had died some years ago, and he lived like a lord. The Archers thought he would be much better for Susan; and told her so, many times. However, she did not like him.
10 She said that if he were ten times as rich, she would rather die than be married to such an ugly man.

And he was ugly, not only in looks, but in his manner too. His
15 legs were short, and his body and hands were long. He had a very large head. He had large eyebrows and nasty, small eyes. His nose looked like a beak, and
20 he had a huge mouth.

George disliked Geoffrey very much. Gibbs hated George because Susan loved him.

As soon as Mr Malcolmson heard that George and
25 Susan were planning to be married, he raised the young man's wages. He also said he would repair a small, old house which belonged to him and let the young couple live there. It was not far from Simon Eade's house.

When Gibbs heard of the coming wedding, he was
30 very angry and jealous. He went at once to see Mr Archer, promising to give Susan a lot of money if she would forget George and marry him instead. Mr Archer would have liked to have been able to make Susan change her mind, but he could not.

Susan was very upset. She told George what had happened, and he was angry.

'Does your father think money is more important than true love?' he said. 'If I thought you would be happier with Gibbs than me, I would give you up at  5 once. But you would be very unhappy with him. He's mean and cruel. He couldn't make any woman happy. I'll work hard for you, Susan, you'll see. We too may have money like his some day.'

'I don't want money, George,' said Susan, 'I'm happy  10 with you the way you are.'

They agreed that, to keep her out of Gibbs's way until the wedding, she should go and stay with her aunt at Orminston. She went away, and so did George. It was nice for him to be away too, for his mother seemed  15 to be growing more against his marriage every day.

## Where is Susan?

When George returned to Cumner he expected to find a letter from Susan waiting for him. He wanted to know when she would be coming back. But there was no  20 letter. Instead, there was a note. It said:

*'George Eade, you are being cheated. Look to G. G.'*

George was worried. He did not feel any better when he found that Gibbs had also left Cumner the  25 day after himself, and was still away.

Next morning, his mother handed him a letter. It was from Susan's aunt. In her letter, she told him that Susan had left her house secretly two days before, and that she was now married to Geoffrey Gibbs.  30

When he read this, George could not believe it. There must be some mistake. It could not be true.

But half an hour later, James Wilkins, Mr Gibbs's servant, brought another letter. It was from Susan, and signed with her new name.

It said:

5     *'I know that you will never forgive me for what I have done. I have behaved very badly to you, and I can't ask you to forgive me. But I do ask you to do nothing about trying to find me, or doing anything to punish anyone. It cannot bring back*
10     *the past. Forget all about me. That's the best thing for both of us. It would have been better if we had never met.'*

He looked at the letter, then, without a word, held it out to his father. He left the room. His parents heard
15 him go up the stairs and lock himself in his bedroom, and they heard no more.

After a while his mother went to him. Although she felt glad that he had not after all married Susan, she knew how he must be feeling.

'Have patience, son,' she said. 'She wasn't good enough for you, you know. I always said so.'

'Mother, I don't want to hear another word about her from now on. What she's done isn't so bad, after all. I'm all right. You won't see any difference in me, at least, not if you'll stop talking about her and using her name, ever again. She's turned my heart to stone, that's all.'

He put his hand on his chest and gave a great sigh. 'This morning I had a living heart here,' he said, 'now it's just a cold, heavy stone. But it doesn't matter.'

'Oh, don't speak like that,' his mother cried. She burst into tears and threw her arms around him. He gently pushed her away, kissed her on the cheek, and led her to the door. 'I must go to work now,' he said, and went down the stairs.

From that day, no one heard him speak of Susan Gibbs. He never spoke of her to his own relations or to hers. Susan appeared to be, for him, as if she had never lived.

### Susan's return

From that awful day, he was a changed man. He worked as hard and carefully as ever, but no man ever saw him smile, or heard him laugh. He stayed away from everyone, except his parents. He was a sad and lonely man.

Mr Geoffrey Gibbs's house beside the Common was rented out to strangers, and for nearly three years nothing was seen of him or his wife. Then news came one day that they were returning to Cumner, and there was soon an air of excitement in the small village. They came back and certain things that had been heard about them over the years were found to be true.

People said that Gibbs treated his wife very badly. Her father and brothers, who had been to visit them more than once, were strangely silent about those visits. It was well known now that Farmer Archer was sorry that his daughter had married Gibbs, even though he had been in favour of the marriage before. No one was surprised when they saw her. She was thin and pale. She hardly ever smiled, except when she played with her little son. He was a lovely, fair-haired child, and looked just like her. But his father was often unkind to him.

It was some time before George met Susan again. He never went out, except to work, and she never left her house except to drive with her husband in his carriage, or to walk to her father's farm. Although George never spoke of her, or watched for her, he could not help hearing things that were said about the Gibbses. The men at work often talked of the husband's cruelty.

One Sunday, the Eades were sitting at the table eating their one o'clock lunch, when they heard the sound of a carriage being driven past. It was going very fast. Mrs Eade went to the window.

'I thought so,' she cried. 'It's Gibbs driving to Tenelms, and he's drunk again. See how he's hitting that horse. And he's got the little boy with him too. He won't be happy until he's broken the child's neck, or his mother's.'

George had also come to the window to see.

'I wish he might break his own neck,' George said, between his teeth.

'Oh, George, don't say such a thing,' cried Mrs Eade, with a pale shocked face.

'Do you think because I'm quiet, that I've forgotten?' cried George. 'Forgotten?' he banged his hand down hard on the table. 'I'll tell you when I shall forget. I shall be lying white and stiff in my coffin. Leave me alone, and it would be best for us all if you never 5 spoke that man's name again.' He went out of the room, and out of the house.

## The accident

It was well known, in the village, that Mrs Gibbs was always afraid for the safety of her son. Her husband 10 was always driving the little boy out in the carriage, far too fast. There had been many ugly scenes between the parents because of this. The more Susan cried and begged him to stop, the worse he became. One day, to frighten her still more, he put the little boy into the 15 carriage alone. He made him stand on the seat with a whip in his hands, while he stood at the door of the carriage, holding the reins loosely in his hand. He was laughing at his wife, who kept begging him to get in, or let her do so. Suddenly there was a bang from a gun in a nearby field.

The horse was frightened, and started off wildly, pulling the reins out of the father's hands. The whip fell from the child's hands on to the back of the horse, making it even more excited. And the boy was thrown
5 screaming to the bottom of the carriage, where he lay still, too frightened to move.

George was close by when all this happened. He threw himself on the flying horse, and held on to its reins with all his strength. He was dragged along,
10 until at last the animal caught its legs in the reins and fell. George was thrown to the ground, but was unhurt except for a few cuts and scratches. The child at the bottom of the carriage, though frightened and screaming, was completely unhurt. In less than five
15 minutes half the village had come to find out what had happened. Susan, holding her child in her arms, came crying up to George.

'Bless you, bless you,' she cried. 'You saved my little boy's life. He might have been killed but for you.
20 How can I ever …'

But a rough hand pushed her aside. 'What are you doing now?' Gibbs was heard to cry. 'Leave that man alone, or I'll … Why are you making a fool of yourself in this way? Look! He has hurt the horse so badly that
25 it will have to be shot.'

The poor girl sat down on the bank and cried, while the people watching shouted out, 'Shame, shame!'

George Eade had turned away from Susan when she rushed up to him. Now, in front of Gibbs he said,
30 'Anyone who shoots that horse of yours will be doing a good deed. And it would be better still if someone would shoot you as they would shoot a mad dog.'

All heard these words. All shook with fear as he spoke them. The anger of the last three years showed
35 in one look of terrible hatred.

## Terrible news

Two days later, Mr Murray, the priest, came to visit
Mrs Eade. He wanted to tell her how pleased he was
that George had not been hurt in the accident. He found
her very worried. George's words had frightened her so       5
badly that she could not sleep. The priest had tried to
talk to George, to get him to come to church, and forget
the hate he felt in his heart, but it was no use. George
answered that as long as he did his work properly and
hurt no one, he had a right to decide for himself things      10
which were his own business. And one of his decisions
was never to go inside a church again.

'It's very sad,' said Mr Murray to Mrs Eade, 'and hard
for you. But have faith. There is something hidden in
this trouble that is good, but we can't see it now.'          15

'It would be strange if I wasn't glad that he had been
unhurt,' said Mrs Eade, 'but it's terrible to have him
looking so full of hate as he does now.'

She stopped talking as there was a knock on the
door. The son of Mr Beach, the butcher, looked in at         20
the door. He looked fearfully from one to the other.

'I don't want any meat this morning, thank you, Jim,'
said Mrs Eade. Then, noticing the look on the young
man's face, she added, 'Are you ill? You look very
strange.'                                                      25

'I don't feel too well,' the boy replied. 'I've just seen
him, and it made me feel sick.'

'Him? Who?'

'Why, haven't you heard? Gibbs has been found dead
in Southanger Woods. He was murdered last night,            30
they say.'

'Gibbs murdered?'

There was a pause of breathless horror.

'They carried his body to the inn, and I saw it.'

Mrs Eade turned very pale. Soon the house was full of people, though why they had come to the Eades's house wasn't quite clear. Everyone was talking about the murder. How had it been done, and why? Into
5  the middle of all the noise and questions walked George Eade.

There was a sudden silence. There was no need to ask if he knew what had happened. His face, pale as death, showed that he had heard the terrible news.
10 But his first words, spoken very softly, were to be remembered for a very long time.

'I wish I'd been found dead in that wood instead of Gibbs.'

## Did George murder Gibbs?

15 There were many reasons why George was thought to have killed Gibbs. His father did not believe that George was guilty, and was sure that it would soon be proved that his son could not have done such a terrible thing. When the police arrived to take George away for
20 questioning, he went without a fuss. He said that he had nothing to fear as he had done nothing wrong.

The body of the dead man had been found at about ten a.m., by a farmer. It lay by the side of a path in the woods. There were signs that there had been a fight.
25 There was blood, too, which must have come from the wound on the back of the dead man's head. He must have been hit from behind by something very heavy. When he was found, he had been dead for about eleven or twelve hours. His pockets were empty, and
30 his money, watch, purse and ring were missing.

Gibbs's two servants said that their master had left the house on the night of the murder at twenty minutes past eight. He had not been drinking. He had said that he would go to the inn first, and then to the Archers' farm. They had not worried when he did not come home that night, because he was often away until morning, and he had a key with him.

Simon Eade and his wife both said that George returned home on the night of the murder, at nine o'clock. He had been out since tea-time, and there was nothing unusual about his looks or speech when he came in. He was with his mother and father until ten, when they all went to bed. His mother had seen him come downstairs in the morning, quite early.

There was a cut on his left hand, which he said had been caused when his knife slipped as he was cutting some bread. There was blood on his coat, which he said he had got on it when he cut his hand. The only thing belonging to the dead man that was found on him was a small pencil, marked with 'G.G.' Job Brettle, one of the villagers, said that Gibbs had used the pencil when he was with him that afternoon. Brettle had noticed the letters on it. George said he had picked it up on the Common, and had no idea whose it was. It was then learned that there had been a very bad quarrel between Mr and Mrs Gibbs on the morning of the murder. After it, she had been heard to say that she could not bear it any more, and would go to someone who would not refuse to help her. She had sent a letter to George Eade, by the son of a villager, and had gone out herself that night, a few minutes after her husband. She had returned fifteen minutes later, and had gone up to her bedroom, and had not left the room until the next morning.

When the judge questioned her about where she had been that night, she would not answer.

George admitted that he had gone to the Southanger Woods at about twenty minutes to eight on the night of the murder, but he refused to give any reason for going there. He had only been about fifteen minutes, he said. He also said that, as he was coming back along the path, he saw Gibbs and his dog coming towards him, but far away. The moon was very bright and he recognized him at once. He didn't want to meet him, so went home another way, reaching the house at about nine o'clock without meeting anyone on the way.

There were now three points in George's favour:

1. *Three people had seen him return home at nine o'clock, and sit down to supper showing no signs of hurry or fear.*

2. *There had not been enough time for him to have done the terrible deed, and hidden any stolen property.*

3. *The good manner in which he had lived up until now.*

The points against him were:

1. *The cut on his hand, and marks of blood on his coat.*

2. *Gibbs's pencil, found on him.*

3. *The fact that he would not say what he had been doing during the thirty minutes that passed between Gibbs leaving the inn, and his (George's) returning home.*

4. *The terrible hate he was known to have felt for the dead man, and certain words he had been heard to speak, showing he wished someone would kill him.*

George stood calmly while all the questions were being asked. He never once let it be seen how he was feeling. It was arranged that he should be properly tried by judge and jury during the next month.

His trial will be remembered for a long time in Cumner. There was a lot of excitement about it, not only in the village, but everywhere around. Mr Malcolmson, who never could believe that George was guilty, spent a lot of money getting good lawyers for him.

George stood calmly in court, looking very much thinner and older. When the court's decision, not guilty, was heard, a great sigh went round the court-room. Silently, George Eade left the court and went home with his father.

People expected that he would leave Cumner after this, and go to live and work somewhere else. But he did not. On the first Sunday after the trial, he went to church. Everyone was very surprised. He had become very quiet in his manner, working hard all day, and reading to himself at night. He never spoke of the past, but he never forgot it.

He and Susan never met. For a long time she was dangerously ill and stayed at her father's house.

## Luke Williams

About twelve months after all these things happened, Mr Murray, the priest, was sitting in his library alone. There was a knock on the door, and a servant came in. He told Mr Murray that a man calling himself Luke Williams wanted to speak with him. It was past ten o'clock, and the priest was ready to go to bed.

'Tell him to come tomorrow morning,' he said. 'It's too late to talk now.'

'I did tell him so, sir, but he said that what he has to say can't wait.'

'Is he a beggar?'

'He didn't ask for anything sir, but he looks very poor.'

'Show him in.'

The man entered. He looked terrible. He was pale, and very thin. He had a nasty cough which made it difficult for him to breathe. He seemed to be very ill. He turned to Mr Murray.

'Well?'

The stranger looked quickly at the servant.

'Leave the room, Robert,' said Mr Murray.

Robert did so, but stayed very close outside.

'This is a strange hour to come to talk to me. Have you something important to say?'

'It is a strange hour, sir, for coming, but my reason for coming is stranger.'

The man turned to the window and looked at the full October moon which lit up the sky.

'Well?' said Mr Murray once more.

But the man's eyes were fixed on the sky.

'Yes,' he said, shaking, 'the moon shone like that on the night of the murder. It shone on Gibbs's face, as he lay there. It shone on his open eyes. I couldn't get them to shut. I've never seen moonlight like that again until tonight. And I'm here to give myself up to you. I always felt I should, and it's better done and over.'

'You murdered Gibbs? You?'

'I did. I've been there tonight, to look at the place. I felt I must see it again. And I saw his eyes, as plain as I see you, open, with the moon shining on them. A horrible sight.'

'You look very wild and ill. Perhaps ...'

'You don't believe me. I wish I didn't believe myself. Look, here.'

With shaking fingers he took from his pocket the watch, purse and ring that had belonged to Gibbs. He laid them on the table, and Mr Murray knew them.

'I used the money,' said the man, faintly. 'There wasn't much, and I needed it badly.'

Then he sat down on a chair. Mr Murray gave him something to drink, and he began to tell his story.

5      He and Gibbs had once worked together in a business. The business had been bad, and Williams had lost all his money. Gibbs had offered to help him, if he would agree to help Gibbs in a plan to steal Susan
10   away from George Eade. When Susan and George had parted for the two weeks before their wedding, Gibbs and Williams had followed her to Ormiston. They had watched her closely. They found out that she was going to spend a day with her cousin, and sent a woman after
15   her with a message. The message was supposed to have come from George. It told her to come quickly to him, as he had been in an accident and was badly hurt. He might only have a few hours to live. The poor girl was so upset, that she followed the woman to a house
20   outside town. When she entered the house, she found Gibbs and Williams waiting for her. They told her it was no use her screaming for help, because she would not be heard. She must promise to marry Gibbs, or she would never be set free. Gibbs added that, if she had
25   married George, he would have had him killed on the way back from the church.

At first Susan refused to agree. But she was watched all day and night, and Gibbs stood over her with a

loaded gun, frightening her so much that she at last
gave in. She wrote the letters to her aunt, and to
George, but was only allowed to put down on paper
what Gibbs told her to say. She was married three
weeks later. Even then, Williams said, she would have 5
refused, but for her fears for George's safety. His life
seemed more important to her than her own happiness.
Then Williams asked for his money.

However, his wicked friend, Gibbs, was not willing
to pay all the money he had promised. He paid some 10
of it, but refused the rest. Williams was in great trouble,
and went down to Cumner, hoping to see Gibbs. He
did see him one night, as Gibbs was driving home
drunk from Tenelms. Gibbs, however, was not too
drunk to recognize Williams, and tried to drive his 15
horse over him.

After that Williams wrote him a very angry letter. In
it he said that Gibbs must bring, on a certain night, to
a certain place in Southhanger Woods, every bit of the
money he had promised to pay. If he failed, then 20
Williams would go to the police the next morning, and
tell them all about the way in which Susan had been
made to marry Gibbs.

Gibbs was frightened by this letter, and went to meet
Williams, but he only took a little money with him. It 25
soon became clear that Gibbs was not going to pay him
anything, so Williams, getting very angry, said he would
take anything Gibbs could give him. A fight began,
during which Gibbs tried to hurt Williams with a knife.
At last, Williams managed to throw Gibbs to the ground. 30
He used such strength that Gibbs's head hit a tree with
such a blow that it killed him. Very frightened by what
he had done, Williams had dragged the body to the
side of the path, taken the things out of the pockets
and run away. The church clock struck ten as he came 35

out of the woods. He walked all that night, rested
the next day, and managed to reach London soon
afterwards, without being discovered. But he was
almost immediately arrested by the police, for debts that
5   he could not pay. He had been in prison until a few
days ago, when he was set free. He was now very ill,
and probably dying.

## A happy ending

This, then, was the story, told in whispers to the priest
10   by that poor man. Before twelve o'clock the next day,
the whole village knew about Williams and what he
had done.

Susan was better now, and able to say that what
Williams had told the priest about her marriage to Gibbs
15   was all true. She also told about the letter she had sent
to George on the day of the murder. It had been to ask
him to go and see her father, and get him to see lawyers
for her. She wanted a separation from her husband, but
was watched too closely to be able to do anything for
20   herself. And as her letters were often opened by her
husband, she asked George to meet her in Southanger
Woods that night to tell her what her father had said.
But Susan, learning that Gibbs was going through the
woods that night, had rushed out to warn George, and
25   prevent the two from meeting, which they very nearly
did.

So once more Susan and George met.

There is a small house by Cumner Common, not far
from Simon Eade's. There you may see Susan, happy
30   now with her new brown-eyed baby in her arms. And
you may also see George Eade, coming in to dinner or
tea, tall and handsome and with a smile on his face.
So, all's well that ends well.

# A Ghost Story

## The two strange men

I cannot explain the story I am about to tell. Nothing quite like it has ever happened to me before, and I hope nothing like it will ever happen again.

A few years ago, it does not matter how many, there was a murder in England which caused great excitement. When the murder was first discovered, no one suspected the man who was afterwards brought to trial. Nothing was said about him in the newspapers at that time, and no one had any idea who he was. It is very important to remember this fact.

One morning at breakfast, I opened my newspaper and found the story about the discovery of the body. I thought it was very interesting, and read it very carefully. I read it twice, if not three times. The body had been discovered in a bedroom.

When I laid down the paper something strange happened to me. It was as if I could see that bedroom clearly before my eyes. It seemed to pass through my room like a picture painted on water. It was so real that I clearly noticed, thankfully, the absence of the dead body from the bed.

I got up and went to the window to get some fresh air, for I felt very strange. As I looked down into the street, my rooms being on the second floor, I noticed two men on the opposite side of the road, walking along one behind the other. The first man often looked back over his shoulder. The second man followed him at a distance of about thirty feet. He had his right hand raised in a threatening way.

First I thought it was strange to make this sort of threatening action in such a public place. Then I thought the fact that no one else seemed to see it was even stranger. Both men made their way among the other people on the street. Nobody that I could see made way for them, touched them or even looked at them. As they passed my windows, they both looked up at me. I saw their faces very clearly, and I knew that I would know them again, anywhere. The first man had an angry look on his face and the second man's face was the colour of grey wax.

## An unexpected visitor

As the days passed, more facts about the murder became known. I tried not to show too great an interest in them, but I did know that the suspected murderer had been sent to prison to wait for his trial.

My sitting-room, bedroom, and dressing-room are all on one floor. There is no way into my dressing-room except through my bedroom. There is a door in it, which used to lead out on to the stairs, but some years ago a bath was put in my dressing-room, and the door had to be closed up because it got in the way. It had been nailed up and covered with wall paper.

I was standing in my bedroom one night, giving some orders for the next day to my servant before he went to bed. My face was towards the only door into my dressing-room, and it was closed. My servant's back was towards that door. While I was speaking to him I saw it open, and a man looked in. He beckoned to me, as if asking me to go to him. I noticed that he looked exactly like the man I had seen in the street whose face was the colour of wax.

The man, having beckoned, drew back and closed the door. At once I picked up a candle and crossed the bedroom. I opened the dressing-room door and looked in. There was nobody there.

I thought that my servant must be surprised by my behaviour. I turned round to him and said, 'Derrick, could you believe that I just thought I saw a …' I put my hand on his arm, and he jumped back. 'Oh yes, sir. A dead man beckoning.'

Now, I do not believe that John Derrick, my trusted servant for more than twenty years, had had any feelings of having seen any such thing, until I touched him. The change in him was so surprising when I touched him, that I am sure he got this feeling about seeing a dead man from me, in some unknown way.

I told him to go and get some wine, and I gave him a glass. I was glad to drink some myself.

I was not very comfortable that night, but, I do not know why, I was sure that the figure would not come back. At daylight I fell into a heavy sleep. I was woken up by John Derrick coming to my bedside with a letter in his hand.

## Called to court

The letter John Derrick brought me had just been delivered to the door. It was an order for me to be on a jury at the next meeting of the Criminal Court of the
5 Old Bailey. I had never been called for jury duty before. I did not know that the murderer was to be tried until I got there.

I sat down with the rest of the people who had been called for jury duty and waited. Soon after, the two
10 judges came in and the court was quiet. An order was given to bring in the prisoner. He appeared, and I knew him at once. It was the first of the two men I had seen going down the street.

If my name had been called then, I don't think I could
15 have answered, I was so surprised. But I was eighth on the list, and by that time I was able to say, 'Here.' I stood up and stepped into the jury box. Now, until then, the prisoner had been watching things calmly, but as soon as I stood up, he seemed to get very worried. He
20 signalled to his lawyer and there was a pause while they whispered together. At last the lawyer shook his head. It was clear that the prisoner did not want me on the jury. I found out later that his first words to the lawyer were, 'You must change that man.' But he would
25 give no reason for it, and said that he had not even known my name until he had heard it called and I stood up. So I stayed where I was in the jury box.

I was chosen as leader of the jury. On the second morning of the trial, after evidence had been taken for
30 about two hours, I sat back and looked at my fellow jurymen. I counted them, but found it very difficult. I counted them several times, yet every time the number was wrong. There should have been twelve, but I made them one too many.

I asked the man sitting next to me to count too. He looked surprised, but turned his head and counted. 'Why,' he said, suddenly, 'we are thirteen … But no, it's not possible. No. We are twelve.' It was very strange.

The jury had to keep together until the end of the trial and a room had been prepared for us at a London inn. We all slept in one large room on separate beds, and we were always watched by an officer, who had promised to look after us carefully. His name was Mr Harker. When we went to sleep at night, Mr Harker's bed was pulled across the door. On the evening of the second day, I did not feel like lying down. I saw Mr Harker sitting on his bed and went over to talk to him. As I sat down beside him he gave a sudden shiver, and said, 'Who is this?'

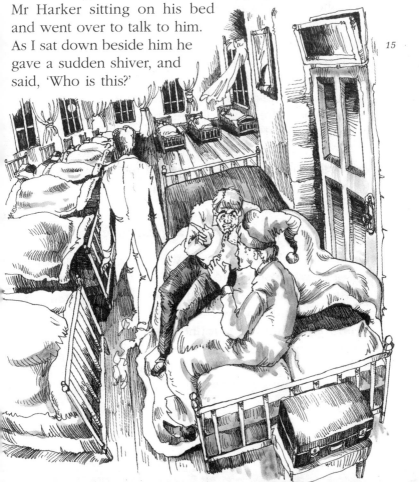

I followed the direction of his eyes, and looking along the room, I saw again the figure I expected. It was the second of the two men who had walked down the street. I got up, walked forward a few steps, then
5   turned back to Mr Harker. He was laughing now. 'I thought for a moment we had a thirteenth juryman, without a bed. But I see now it was only the moonlight,' he said. I turned again. The man was still there.

I did not say anything to Mr Harker about the man,
10   but asked him to take a walk with me to the end of the room. I watched what the stranger did. He stood for a few minutes by the bed of each juryman, close to the pillow. He always went to the right side of the bed and stood just looking down thoughtfully. He took no
15   notice of me, or of my bed, which was nearest to Mr Harker's. Then he seemed to leave through a high window, where the moonlight was coming in.

Next morning at breakfast, it seemed that everyone present had dreamed of the murdered man, except
20   myself and Mr Harker.

I was now sure that the second man who had gone down the street was the murdered man. It was as clear to me as if he had told me so himself.


## More ghostly appearances

25   On the fifth day of the trial, when the case against the prisoner was coming to an end, a small picture of the murdered man was offered as evidence. It had been missing from the room at the time when the body had been found. But it was found later in a place where the
30   murderer had been seen digging. It was shown to the judges first, and then handed to an officer of the court to take to the jury. As the officer was bringing the picture across to me, the figure of the second man

suddenly appeared. It snatched the picture from the officer and gave it to me with its own hands. At the same time it said in a low, frightening voice, 'I was younger then, and my face was not so white.' It then came between me and the next juryman as I was about to give him the picture, and between him and the juryman as he was about to pass it on. And so it passed the picture on through the whole of our jury and back to me. None of the others, however, noticed anything wrong.

On the fifth day, the case against the prisoner was closed.

Of course, as we were shut up together, the jurymen and I talked a great deal about the case. We now knew the facts about it, and our talk was very serious. Among the jurymen there was one whom I thought very stupid. He had two followers, and the three of them seemed to think that the prisoner might not have done the murder at all. At about midnight, when the three of them were talking very loudly, I again saw the murdered man. He stood behind them, beckoning to me. When I went towards them and began to talk to them, he went away.

This was the beginning of a separate set of appearances, which happened in that room. Whenever a group of my fellow jurymen got together talking, he would appear amongst them. Whenever they seemed to be talking against him, he would beckon to me.

It must be remembered that until the fifth day of the trial, when the picture of the murdered man was shown to the jury, I had never seen the ghost in court. Then, as the case for the defence began, it was in the court-room every day. However, it did not take any notice of me now but always stood by the person who was talking at the time. For example, the throat of the

murdered man had been cut
straight across. In the opening
speech for the defence, it was
suggested that the dead man might have cut his own
5   throat. At that very moment, the figure, with its throat
in the terrible condition just described, stood at the
speaker's elbow. It made movements across its wind-
pipe, now with the right hand, now with the left, to
show how impossible it would have been to make that
10   wound by itself. For another example, a woman was
called to give evidence that the prisoner was a good
man. The figure at that time stood on the floor in front
of her, looking her full in the face. It pointed to the
prisoner's evil face.
15      I had noticed something else about these appearances, too. While it was clear that the people could not

see the figure, they showed signs of feeling very
uncomfortable when it was near them. The person who
suggested that the man had killed himself, began to feel
too warm, and stopped to wipe his forehead several
times. The woman's eyes certainly did follow the
figure's pointing finger, and she looked troubled when
she looked towards the prisoner's face.

On the eighth day of the trial, after the break which
was taken every afternoon for a few minutes rest, I
came back into court with the rest of the jury, a little
while before the return of the judges. I stood up and
looked round. I thought the figure had gone, until I
looked to the seats upstairs. There it was, leaning over
a woman's shoulder to see if the judges were back or
not. Immediately afterwards, that woman screamed,
fainted, and was carried out. The same thing happened
to one of the judges. When the case was over, and he
sat back to read all the evidence, the murdered man
entered by the judge's door, came to the judge's desk,
and looked eagerly over his shoulder at the pages of
notes that he was reading. A change came over the
judge's face, his hand stopped turning the pages, the
strange shiver that I knew so well passed over him. His
voice sounded weak. 'Excuse me, gentlemen,' he said.
'I don't feel very well. It must be the air in here.' And
he did not recover until he had drunk a glass of water.

## The end of the case

Through all those ten long days of the trial, with the
same people in the court, the same fog outside, the
same rain falling from the same grey skies, the
murdered man remained clear in my eyes. I never once
saw him look at the prisoner. Again and again I
wondered 'Why doesn't he?' But he never did.

And he never looked at me again after the picture was shown, not, at least, until the closing minutes of the trial arrived. At seven minutes to ten at night, we, the jury, went out to decide if the prisoner was guilty or not. The three members of the jury, whom I mentioned before were not sure, gave us a lot of trouble. But nine of us had made our decision, and at last, after going over a few points again, the others agreed. We returned to the court at ten past twelve.

The murdered man stood opposite the jury box, on the other side of the court. As I took my place, his eyes rested on me with great attention. He seemed satisfied, and slowly shook a great grey cloth, which he carried, over his head and body. As, I gave our decision, 'Guilty,' the cloth fell down, all was gone, and his place was empty.

The murderer was asked by the judge if he had anything to say before the sentence of death was passed on him. He whispered something which was described in the newspaper next day as a few words that made no sense; something about not having had a fair trial.

What he had really said was this:

'My Lord, I knew I was a dead man when I saw the leader of the jury. My Lord, I knew he would never let me off, because, before the police caught me, he somehow got to my bedside in the night, woke me, and put a rope round my neck.'

# THE SIGNALMAN

## A worried man

'Hello, below there.'

He heard the voice calling to him. He was standing at the door of his signal-box. There was a flag in his hand, folded round its short stick. Surely he knew where the voice came from? But instead of looking up to where I stood at the top of the steep bank, he turned and looked along the railway line. There was something strange in the way he did this, though I could not have said what.

'Hello, below.'

From looking down the line, he turned around again, and, raising his eyes, saw me high above him.

'Is there a path by which I can come down and speak to you?' I shouted.

He looked up at me without replying. Just then the earth began to shake, and a rush of air made me jump back. It was a train.

When the steam from the train had passed, I looked down again. The man was now re-folding the flag he had shown when the train went by. I repeated my question. After a short pause, he pointed with his flag to a spot on the bank about two hundred yards from where I stood. I called 'All right,' and made my way to that point. I found a rough path leading down. It was very steep and dangerous. When I was half-way down, I looked for the man again. He was standing between the rails on the side where the train had just passed. He seemed lost in thought. I continued down the path,

and at last reached the bottom. As I drew near I saw that the man was very pale, with a dark beard and eyebrows. This place, where he worked, was very lonely and dark. On each side was a wall of rough
5    stone, so he had nothing interesting to look at except for a strip of sky above. In one direction the railway lines stretched on and on between the walls, and in the other, they disappeared into the great black mouth of a tunnel. There was a red light just outside the tunnel
10    entrance. The sunlight hardly ever found its way down here, and there was a nasty, dead smell all around. It was cold too, for the wind rushed through along the line. I felt that I had left the normal world behind.

Before the man moved, I was almost near enough to
15    touch him. He did not take his eyes from my face, but stepped back one step, and lifted his hand.

'This is a very lonely place to work,' I said. 'It looked so interesting from where I stood, up on top, that I felt I must come down and talk to you. I suppose you don't get many visitors?' He did not reply. Instead, he looked hard at the red light near the tunnel entrance. He looked all round it, as if searching for something, then he looked back at me. 5

'You look after that light, I expect,' I said.

He answered in a low voice, 'Don't you know what I do?' 10

I suddenly felt that this man was not real. He seemed more like a ghost than a normal human being. The thought made me step back, and I noticed he was looking at me fearfully.

'You look at me as if you were afraid of me,' I said, 15 trying to smile.

'I thought I had seen you before,' he answered.

'Where?' I asked.

He pointed to the red light he had looked at.

'There?' I said. 'My good man, what would I be doing 20 there? However, I never was there, you may believe that.'

'I think I may,' he said, slowly. 'Yes, I think I may.'

His manner changed now, and he became more friendly. I asked him many questions, and found out 25 that his work was not hard, but was very important for the safety of the trains. He had to change the signal, look after the lights and turn an iron handle now and again. He had spent many of his lonely hours in learning a foreign language, and teaching himself 30 mathematics. He had never been much good at learning at school.

I asked him if he always had to stay down here when he was on duty. Was he sometimes able to get up into the fresh air at the top of the steep bank? He replied 35 that, yes, he sometimes went up to the top, if there were not many trains running. But he was always having to listen for the bell in his signal-box, and didn't like to go too far in case he missed it.

5     He took me into his box where there was a fire, a desk for a large book, a telegraphic instrument with a dial and needles, and the little bell he had just spoken about.

We sat and talked. The little bell rang several times
10  and he had to read off messages and send replies. Once he had to stand outside the door and show his flag while a train went by. He seemed to do his job carefully. Twice, however, he broke off speaking to me, and with a pale face, looked at the little bell when it
15  did NOT ring. He then opened the door of the box and looked towards the red light near the mouth of the tunnel. Both times he came back to the fire looking rather worried and a little frightened.

When the time came for me to leave, I thanked him
20  and said, 'You seem to be quite happy, working down here.'

'I used to be, sir,' he replied, 'but I am worried, sir, I am worried.'

'What about?' I asked. 'What is the trouble?'

25  'It is very difficult to explain, sir. It is very hard to speak of. If you ever visit me again I will try to tell you.'

'But I certainly mean to come and see you again,' I replied. 'When shall I come?'

30  'I finish early in the morning and I shall be here again at ten tomorrow night, sir.'

'I will come at eleven.'

He thanked me, and we went outside.

'I'll show my white light, sir,' he said in his strange
35  low voice, 'till you have found the way up. When you

have found it, don't call out. And when you are at the top, don't call out.'

I thought this strange but said, 'Very well.'

'And when you come down tomorrow night, don't call out. Let me ask you a last question. What made you cry out, "Hello, below there," tonight?'

'Heaven knows, I cried something like that …' I said.

'Not like that, sir. Those were the very words. I know them well.'

'Well, if I said those words, it was, no doubt, because I saw you below.'

'For no other reason, sir?'

'What other reason could I possibly have?'

'You don't feel that you were made to say those words in some strange way?'

'No.'

He wished me goodnight, and held up his light. I walked back down the railway line, with the very nasty feeling that there was a train coming behind me, and found the path. It was easier going up than it had been to come down, and I got back to my hotel without any trouble.

## My second visit

The next night, I started down the path at exactly eleven o'clock. He was waiting for me at the bottom, with his white light on.

'I have not called out,' I said, when we came close together. 'May I speak now?'

'Of course, sir.'

'Good evening, then.'

'Good evening, sir,' he replied, shaking my hand. We walked side by side to his box, entered it, closed the door, and sat down by the fire.

'I have made up my mind to tell you what troubles me,' he said, speaking softly. 'I thought you were someone else yesterday evening. That troubles me.'

'The mistake?'

'No. The "someone else".'

'Who is it?'

'I don't know.'

'He looks like me?'

'I don't know. I never see the face. The left arm is across the face, and the right arm is waving. *Violently* waving. This way.'

I watched him, as he waved his arm. It was like, I thought, someone signalling 'For God's sake clear the way!'

'One night,' said the man, 'I was sitting here, when I heard a voice cry, "Hello, below there." I jumped up and looked out of the door. There was a full moon, and it was quite easy to see. I saw this person standing by the red light near the tunnel, waving just like I showed you.

The voice seemed rough with shouting, and it cried, "Look out! Look out!" And then again, "Hello, below there! Look out!" I caught up my lamp, turned it on red, and ran towards the figure, calling, "What's wrong? What has happened? Where?" It stood just outside the black entrance to the tunnel. I went so close to it that I wondered why it kept its sleeve across its eyes. I ran right up to it, and had my hand stretched out to pull the sleeve away, when it was gone.'

'Into the tunnel?' I asked.

'No. It just disappeared. I ran on into the tunnel. I stopped and held my lamp high. There was no one there. I ran out again, feeling very frightened. I looked all around the red light with my own red light, and I went up the iron ladder to the platform at the top. I came down again, and ran back here. I telegraphed both ways, "Is anything wrong there?" The answer came back, both ways, "No, all is well".'

I tried to tell him that he must have imagined the figure, and that the cry he had heard must have been made by the wind blowing through the telegraph wires.

'Just listen to it, now,' I said.

We sat listening for a while, but he said he knew that sound well, and the cry was not like that at all. Also, he had not finished his story.

## A terrible shock

'Just six hours after that strange appearance, a terrible accident happened on the line. Only ten hours later, the dead and those who had been hurt were brought through the tunnel over the spot where the figure had stood.'

A horrible shiver went down my back. It was indeed most strange. But he had still more to tell.

'That was just a year ago,' he said, laying his hand on my arm. 'Six or seven months passed, and I had recovered from the surprise and shock, when one morning, at dawn, I looked out of the door towards the red light, and saw that figure again.'

'Did it cry out?' I asked.

'No. It was silent.'

'Did it wave its arm?'

'No. It leaned against the post of the light, with both hands in front of its face. Like this.'

Once more I watched as he covered his face. It was an act of great sadness. I had seen statues standing like that in graveyards.

'Did you go up to it?'

'I came in and sat down, because I felt ill. When I went to the door again, it was daylight, and the ghost had gone.'

'But did nothing happen after this?'

He touched me on the arm, and nodded.

'That very day, as a train came out of the tunnel, I noticed somebody waving at a carriage window on my side. I saw it just in time to signal the driver to stop. He shut off the engine, and put his brake on, but the train ran on for a hundred yards or more. I ran after it, and as I went along, I heard terrible screams and cries. A beautiful young lady had died suddenly in the train, and was brought in here and laid down on this floor where we are sitting.'

I jumped up and looked down at the floor, then up at him.

'It's true, sir. Exactly as it happened.'

I couldn't think of anything to say, and my mouth was very dry.

He continued talking.

'Now, sir, listen to this. Then perhaps you will

understand why I am so troubled. The ghost came back, a week ago. Ever since, it has been there, now and again.'

'At the light?'

'Yes. At the danger-light.'

'What does it seem to do?'

He repeated that first action of the arm waving. Then he went on. 'I have no peace or rest. It calls to me for many minutes together, "Below there! Look out! Look out!" It stands waving to me. It rings the little bell on the telegraph.'

'Did it ring your bell yesterday evening when I was here, and you went to the door?'

'Twice.'

'Now, look,' I said. 'I was watching the bell, and my ears were open, and I am quite sure that it did NOT ring at those times. No, nor at any other time, except when it was rung by someone at the station, trying to get in touch with you.'

He shook his head. 'I have never made a mistake like that, sir. The ghost's ring is quite different from that

of a normal man. And I have never noticed the bell
move, when he rings it. I am not surprised that you
failed to hear. But I heard it.'

'And did the ghost seem to be there when you
looked out?'

'It WAS there.'

'Both times?'

'Yes, both times.'

'Will you come to the door with me, and look for it
now?'

He bit his lower lip, as if he did not want to go
outside, but he got up. I opened the door, and stood
on the step, while he stood in the doorway. There was
the danger-light. There was the great black mouth of
the tunnel. There were the high wet stone walls, and
there were the stars above them.

'Do you see it?' I asked, looking carefully at his face.
His eyes turned towards the spot.

'No,' he answered. 'It is not there.'

'I agree,' I said.

We went in again and shut the door.

'You will understand, sir, that what troubles me so
much is what does the ghost mean? What is it warning
me about? What is the danger? Where is the danger?
There is danger somewhere on the line. Something
terrible will happen, I am sure. Look at what happened
before. But this is very cruel to me. What can I do?'

He took out his handkerchief and wiped his forehead.

'If I telegraph "Danger", I can give no reason for it.
I should get into trouble, and do no good. They would
think I was mad. This is the way it would work:
Message: "Danger: Take care." Answer: "What danger?
Where?" Message: "Don't know. But for God's sake
take care!" They would dismiss me. What else could
they do?'

I felt very sorry for him.

'When the figure first stood under the danger light,' he went on, 'why didn't it tell me where the accident was to happen, if it must happen? Why not tell me how to stop it? When it came the second time and hid its face, why not tell me "She is going to die. Let them keep her at home"? If it came on those two days, only to show me that what it had said was true, and so prepare me for the third, why not warn me plainly now? And why me? I'm only a poor signalman. Why not go to someone more important, who would have power to do something about it?'

I could not answer him. But I tried to calm him. It was important that he should try to forget the appearances, and settle down to do his job properly. The safety of the people travelling on the trains was in his hands. I offered to stay with him through the night, but he would not let me. So I left at two in the morning.

As I went back up the steep path, I paused once or twice to look at the red light. I did not like the way those two terrible things had happened, so soon after the appearance of the ghost. But what should I do? It would be unfair of me to go and tell his manager about all this. But I knew something would have to be done, or the man would go mad.

I decided at last to offer to go with him to see a good doctor. We would. see what he thought about this business. The man had told me that he would be off duty during the next day, but would start work again just after sunset. I had promised to go to see him then.

## A sad ending

Next evening was a lovely evening, and I walked out early to enjoy it. The sun was not quite down when I crossed the fields towards the railway lines. I decided to go for a longer walk, half an hour there, and half an hour back. Then it would be time to go down to the signalman's box.

Before I started off, however, I stepped to the edge of the bank and looked down from the same point where I had first seen him. I cannot describe the terrible feeling that came over me when, close to the tunnel, I saw something that looked like a man, with his left sleeve over his eyes, violently waving his right arm.

The terrible feeling of fear left me, for looking more closely, I saw that this was indeed a human being. He seemed to be showing his actions to a group of men who stood nearby. The danger light was not yet lit. Beside it was a little low hut which I had not seen before. It looked no bigger than a bed.

I knew at once that something was wrong, and blamed myself for leaving the man there alone with no one to look after him and see what he was doing. I went down the path as quickly as I could.

'What is the matter?' I asked the men.

'A signalman was killed this morning.'

'Not the man who works in this signal-box?'

'Did you know him, sir? Come and see,' the man replied.

'Oh! How did this happen, how did this happen?' I asked, turning from one to another.

'He was knocked down by a train, sir. No man in England knew his job better than he did. But somehow he was not clear of the rail. It was just daylight, and he had put out the light. He had his lamp in his hand. As the engine came out of the tunnel he had his back towards it, and it knocked him down. That man drove the engine, and was showing us how it happened. Show the gentleman, Tom.'

The engine driver stepped back to his place at the mouth of the tunnel.

'As I came round the bend in the tunnel, sir,' he said, 'I saw him at the end. There was no time to stop, and I knew he was a very careful man. He didn't seem to hear the whistle, and I shut it off as we were nearly on top of him. I called to him as loudly as I could.'

'What did you say?'

'I said, "Hello, below there! Look out! Look out! For God's sake clear the way!"'

I shivered.

'Ah! It was a terrible time, sir. I never stopped calling to him. I put this arm in front of my eyes, so as not to see, and I waved this arm to the end. But it was no good.'

As I close this strange story, I would just like to point out one thing. It is a fact that the warning that the engine driver gave included not only the words which the poor signalman had told me he had heard. It also included the words which I had added in my own mind to the actions he had shown me.

# 5

# THE BARON OF GROGZWIG

## The Baron wants a change

The Baron lived in an old castle in Germany. He came from a good family, and was quite rich. He was a fine tall man, with black hair, and a great black beard. He wore a jacket and trousers made of the finest green cloth, and red leather boots. He always had a trumpet hanging from his shoulder, and when he blew it, twenty-four other gentlemen, all dressed in the same coloured cloth, came to him at once. Then they and the Baron would go out to hunt the wild pig, or perhaps a bear. They spent many happy days and nights drinking and eating with the Baron. It was all great fun.

But after a while the Baron began to get tired of his friends. He felt he needed a change from sitting down to dinner with the same twenty-four men, always talking about the same things, and telling the same stories. He began quarrelling with them. He tried kicking two or three of them every night after dinner. This was a pleasant change at first, but it became boring after a week or so, and the Baron began to look around for another way in which to amuse himself.

One night, after he and his friends had been out bear hunting, the Baron sat at the top of his table, looking very unhappy. He swallowed huge glasses of wine, but the more he swallowed, the sadder he looked.

Suddenly he jumped up.

'I will,' he cried, hitting the table with his hand. 'Gentlemen, fill your glasses, and drink to the Lady of Grogzwig.'

Twenty-four glasses were raised, and down twenty-four throats went twenty-four pints of the best white wine. 5

'I shall go to Baron Von Swillenhausen tomorrow and demand that he gives me his daughter in marriage. If he refuses, I will cut off his nose.' 10

Baron Von Swillenhausen was lucky that he had a good and sensible daughter. 15 She did not refuse the Baron of Grogzwig, and there was much feasting and merry-making.

For six weeks, the wild pigs and the bears had a holiday. The Baron's men had a wonderful time, eating 20 and drinking, but sad to say, their happy days were almost at an end.

## From bad to worse

'My dear,' said the Baroness one day.

'My love,' said the Baron. 25

'Those terrible, noisy men.'

'Which, madam?' said the Baron, jumping up.

The Baroness pointed out of the window to where the Baron's men were having a drink before setting out to hunt a pig or two. 30

'Those are my huntsmen, madam,' said the Baron.

'Send them away,' whispered the Baroness.

'Send them away!' cried the Baron in surprise.

'To please me, my love,' replied the Baroness.

'To please the devil, madam,' answered the Baron.

The Baroness gave a great cry, and fainted at the Baron's feet.

5 What could he do? He called for his wife's maid, and sent for the doctor. Then he rushed into the yard, kicked two of his men, and gave them all orders to go.

From then on, things went from bad to worse. Day by day, and year by year, the Baroness changed things 10 in the castle. So by the time he was a fat fellow of forty-eight, the Baron had no feasting, fun, or huntsmen to amuse him. Instead he had a house full of children. For each year, for twelve years, the Baroness gave him a son or a daughter. His wife's family had taken 15 a dislike to him, and he got into debt and lost nearly all his money.

'I don't see what I can do to make things any better,' said the Baron to himself. I think I'll kill myself. That is what I'll do: I'll commit suicide.'

20 This, he thought, was a good idea. The Baron took an old hunting knife from a cupboard nearby, and sharpened it on his boot. Then he pointed it at his throat.

'Hm,' he said, 'perhaps it is not sharp enough.'

25 He sharpened it again, and had another try, but just at that moment there was a loud scream from the room upstairs where his children were playing.

'If I was unmarried,' sighed the Baron, 'I could have done it fifty times by now.'

30 He called to a servant, and asked for a bottle of wine and a pipe to be placed in the small room behind the hall. Half an hour later, the Baron went to the little room. It looked very comfortable, for there was a fire burning brightly, and his wine and pipe stood ready 35 on a table.

## An unexpected guest

'Leave the lamp,' said the Baron to his servant.

'Anything else, my lord?' asked the servant.

'No, thank you. You may go.'

The servant left the room, and the Baron locked the door. 5

'I'll smoke a last pipe,' said the Baron, 'then I'll be off.'

So, putting the knife on the table till he wanted it, the Baron filled his glass with the wine, and sat down to enjoy his last pipe. 10

He thought about a great many things. About his present troubles and past days of happiness. He thought about the huntsmen who were all in different parts of the country. He was thinking of wild pigs and bears, when he raised his eyes and found, to his great surprise, 15 that he was not alone.

No, he was not, for, on the opposite side of the fire someone else was sitting. It was a terrible figure, with deep red eyes, and a very long, thin face. He had thick black hair. His coat was blue, 20 and fastened down the front with coffin handles. The legs of his trousers were covered with metal name-plates from coffins.

He took no notice of the Baron, but sat looking into the fire.

'Hello!' said the Baron, loudly, and stamped his foot to get his attention.

'Hello!' replied the stranger, moving his eyes towards the Baron, but not his face or himself. 'What now?'

'What now! replied the Baron. 'I should ask that question. How did you get in here?'

'Through the door,' replied the figure.

'What are you?' asked the Baron.

'A man,' replied the figure.

'I don't believe it,' said the Baron.

'Don't then,' said the figure.

'I won't,' said the Baron.

The figure looked at the Baron for some time, then said, 'I see I can't fool you. I'm not a man.'

'What are you then?' asked the Baron.

'I am the Ghost of Sorrow and Suicide,' said the figure. As he spoke, he turned towards the Baron. The Baron could see that he had a long piece of wood running through the centre of his body. The figure pulled this out, and laid it on the table, with no more fuss than if it had been a walking stick.

'Now,' said the figure, looking over to the hunting knife, 'are you ready for me?'

'Not quite,' replied the Baron. 'I must finish this pipe first.'

'Be quick, then,' said the figure.

'You seem to be in a hurry,' said the Baron.

'Why, yes, I am,' answered the figure. 'There are lots of people waiting for me all over England and France at the moment, and I am very busy.'

'Do you drink?' said the Baron, touching the bottle with the end of his pipe.

'Nine times out of ten,' said the figure.

## 'Why should I do it?'

The Baron took another good look at his new friend.
He was certainly a very strange person. At last, he asked
him if he ever helped people to commit suicide.

'No,' said the figure, 'but I am always there.'                    5

'Just to see it is done correctly, I suppose?' said the
Baron.

'Just that,' said the figure. 'Be as quick as you can, will
you. There is a young gentleman who has too much
money and too much time to waste, waiting for me now.'    10

'Going to kill himself because he's got too much
money?' said the Baron, quite amused. 'Ha! ha! that's a
good one.' (This was the first time that the Baron had
laughed for a long time).

'I say,' cried the figure, looking very frightened, 'don't    15
do that again.'

'Why not?' asked the Baron.

'Because it gives me a pain all over my body,' replied
the figure. 'Sigh as much as you like, that does me
good.'                                                             20

Without thinking, the Baron sighed at the mention of
the word, and the figure looked better. It took the
hunting knife and handed it to the Baron.

'It's not a bad idea though,' said the Baron, feeling
the edge of the knife. 'A man killing himself because    25
he has too much money.'

'Pooh!' said the ghost, 'no better than a man's killing
himself because he has none or little.'

Whether the ghost knew what he was saying, or
whether he thought that the Baron's mind was so made    30
up that nothing would change it, I don't know. I only
know that the Baron stopped his hand, all of a sudden,
opened his eyes wide, and looked as if new life had
come into him for the very first time.

'Why, of course,' he said, 'nothing is so bad that it can't be made better again.'

'Except an empty purse,' said the ghost.

'Even that. It may one day be filled again,' said the Baron.

'Scolding wives,' cried the ghost.

'Oh, they may be quietened,' said the Baron.

'Twelve children,' shouted the ghost.

'Can't all go wrong, surely,' said the Baron.

The ghost was getting very angry with the Baron, and told him that when he had finished joking, he would be happy if he got on with killing himself.

'But I am not joking,' said the Baron.

'Then hurry up,' said the ghost. 'Leave this terrible life at once.'

'I don't know,' said the Baron, playing with the knife. 'It's not a very happy one certainly, but I'm not sure that yours is any better. How do I know that I shall be any better off when I have left this world?'

'Hurry up!' screamed the ghost.

'Keep away!' said the Baron. 'I'm not going to feel sorry for myself any more. I shall go and speak to the Baroness first. Then I'll try the fresh air and the bears again.' He fell back into his chair, laughing.

The figure stood up and moved back a step or two, looking at the Baron with great fear. When the laughing stopped, the ghost caught up the piece of wood, pushed it hard into its body, gave a terrible scream, and disappeared.

The Baron never saw it again. He made up his mind to give life another try, and soon had the Baroness and her family doing what he wanted. He died many years later, not a rich man, but certainly a very happy one.

# BLACK COLL
# AND THE DEVIL'S INN

## Unpleasant strangers

This is the story of a man who lived in the house called the Devil's Inn. It stands in a small valley in the Connemara mountains in Ireland. The man who built it was a stranger. No one knew where he had come from, and the people living nearby gave him the name Black Coll. They called his house the Devil's Inn. No one had ever been known to enter the house as a friend, and Black Coll lived alone except for an old servant. They were an unpleasant pair.

During the first year that they lived in the valley, many people tried to guess who they were. Some said that Black Coll was a member of the family who had once owned land there. They thought he had come to try to get his land back. Others said he had done something very wrong, and thought he might have run away from another country. But no one really knew anything about the two men, and when two years had passed, the people began to forget that they were there.

By climbing one of the mountains near his home, Black Coll could look down and see a big old house. It had been empty for many years, but one day he saw that it was being repaired and painted. He learned that the new owner of the land in that part of the country was coming to live there. His name was Colonel Blake.

It was autumn when Colonel Blake, his only daughter, and a party of friends came to the house. Now the house was full of life and laughter, but Black Coll was no longer interested in watching it from his mountain top. He kept away from the house, and from the people who were living there.

One evening in September the wind changed, and in half an hour the mountains were covered in thick cloud. Black Coll was far from his home, but he knew the mountain paths so well that he was not frightened by bad weather. But while he was walking along he heard a cry. He quickly followed the sound, and came to a man who was completely lost and in danger of death at every step.

'Follow me,' said Black Coll to this man. In an hour he had brought him safely down to the house he used to look at.

## The Colonel's daughter

'I am Colonel Blake,' said the man when they at last stood under the lighted windows of the house. 'Please tell me quickly to whom I owe my life.'

'Colonel Blake,' said Black Coll, after a strange silence, 'your father made my father lose all his money and land at a game of cards. Both of them are dead now, but you and I are alive, and I have promised myself that I will kill you. My name is Coll. They call me "Black" Coll.'

The Colonel laughed at Black Coll's unhappy face.

'And you began to keep your promise tonight by saving my life,' he said. 'Come, I am a soldier, and I know how to meet an enemy. But I would far rather meet a friend, and I shall not be happy until you have eaten a meal with us. It is my daughter's birthday, please come in and join us.'

Black Coll looked down at the ground.

'I have told you who and what I am,' he said, 'and I will not come into your house.'

At that moment a door opened near them and a girl appeared. She was quite tall and dressed in white silk. Her face was as pale as her dress. There were lovely white pearls around her throat, and red roses in her hair. Black Coll had never seen anything more beautiful.

Evleen Blake went up to her father.

'Thank God you are safe,' she said. 'The others have been home for an hour.'

'My dear, I owe my life to this brave gentleman,' said the Colonel. 'Try to make him come in and be our guest. He wants to return to the mountains and lose himself again in the clouds where he found me.'

'I beg you to come in, sir,' said Evleen. 'If you had not found my father, this night of happiness would have been turned into sorrow.' She held out her hand to the tall man. He took it and held it tightly. The proud girl's eyes flashed with surprise, for his strength had hurt her. Was this Black Coll mad, or rude?

The guest no longer refused to enter, and followed the girl into a little room where a lamp was burning. Now they could all see clearly. Evleen looked at the stranger's dark face, and felt great fear and dislike.

So Black Coll was present at Evleen Blake's birthday party. Here he was, under a roof that should have been his own. Here he was, having waited for years for the chance to kill the man who had been the cause of so much unhappiness. His mother had died of a broken heart, his father had killed himself, his brothers and sisters had all gone away. Here he stood, like Samson without his strength, all because of this lovely girl who looked so beautiful in white silk and red roses.

## One red rose

5   Evleen moved among her guests, trying not to notice those strange eyes which followed her everywhere. Her father asked her to be kind to the man who had saved his life. She took him to a room with many old paintings on the walls, and talked about them to him. She showed
10   him many works of art, trying to move his attention from herself. But it did not matter what she said, he still kept his eyes on her. They stopped for a moment by an open window. Through it they could look out towards the sea. The full moon was high up in the sky.
15   'My father planned this window himself,' said the girl. 'Don't you think it is well made?'

Black Coll did not reply to her question, but suddenly asked her for a rose from a small bunch she had fastened to the front of her dress.

20   For the second time that night Evleen Blake's eyes flashed in angry surprise. But this man had saved her father's life. She broke off a flower and held it out to him. He took the rose, and also the hand that gave it, and covered it with kisses.

25   'Sir,' she cried angrily, 'if you are a gentleman you must be mad. If you are not mad, then you are not a gentleman.'

'Be kind to me,' said Black Coll, 'I love you. I have never loved a woman before. Ah,' he cried, as a look
30   of dislike crept over her face, 'you hate me. You were afraid the first time your eyes met mine. I love you, and you hate me.'

'I do,' cried Evleen. 'Please, don't talk like this again.'

'I won't trouble you any longer,' said Black Coll. And walking to the window, he placed one strong hand on the edge, and jumped out of her sight.

## The Burrag-bos

All through that night Black Coll walked in the mountains, but not towards his own home. He had not eaten since the morning before, and at sunrise was glad to see a small house. He walked in and asked for water to drink and a place where he might rest.

There had been a death in the house, and the kitchen was full of people. They had come to watch over the body all night and to pray. Many were asleep, but those who were awake crossed themselves when they heard Black Coll's evil name. But an old man invited him in and gave him some milk, promising some food later. He took him to a small room at the back of the kitchen. In the room were two women sitting by the fire, and at one end a small bed.

'A traveller,' said the old man to the two women, and they nodded their heads. Black Coll went to the bed and lay down.

The women stopped talking for a while, but when they thought that the visitor was asleep they began again. There was only a tiny window in the room, but Black Coll could see the two women in the light of the fire. One was very old, the other quite a young girl.

'It's the funniest marriage I ever heard of,' the girl said. 'Only three weeks ago, he was telling everyone that he hated her like poison.'

'I know,' said the old woman, 'but he could not help himself, poor man. She put the Burrag-bos on him.'

'The what?' asked the girl.

'The Burrag-bos.'

'But what is it?' asked the girl, eagerly. 'What's the Burrag-bos, and where did she get it?'

'I shouldn't tell you, you're too young, but listen. It's a strip of the skin from a dead body. It must be taken from the top of the head to the heel without a break, or it will not work. Then it is rolled up and put on a piece of string round the neck of the one you want. It makes him fall in love with you.'

The girl was looking at her friend in horror.

'How terrible,' she cried. 'No one on earth would dare to do such a bad thing.'

'Well, there is one person who does it, and that's Pexie. Haven't you ever heard of her?'

The girl nodded. 'She lives up in the hills,' she whispered.

'Well, she will do it for money any day.'

'Sh,' whispered the girl, 'the traveller is getting up. What a short rest he has had.'

It was enough for Black Coll, however. He had got up, and now made his way back to the kitchen. The old man was there, and had some food ready for the traveller. When he had eaten, Black Coll set off for the mountains again, just as the sun was rising. By sunset he was walking in the hills looking for Pexie's house.

## The witch

He found her at last in a tiny broken-down hut. She was an ugly old woman. Her black hair stuck out from under a dirty red scarf which was tied round her head. She was bending over a pot upon her fire, and she gave Black Coll an evil look as he came near.

He told her what he wanted.

'Ah, the Burrag-bos. But I'll want some money. The Burrag-bos is hard to get.'

'I will pay,' said Black Coll, and he put some money down on her table.

The old witch fell on it, and laughing, she gave her visitor a look which made even Black Coll feel frightened.

'You're a fine man,' she said, 'and I will get you the Burrag-bos. But you have not paid enough. More, more.'

She stretched out her claw-like hand, and Black Coll dropped some more money into it. She screamed with happiness.

'Now, listen to me,' said Black Coll. 'I have paid you well, but if your devil's charm does not work, I will have you hunted down and killed as a witch.'

'Work,' cried Pexie, rolling up her eyes. 'Of course it will work. Even if she hates you now, this charm will make her love you like her own soul before the sun sets or rises. That, or the girl will go mad before one hour is up.'

'You made that last part up,' cried Black Coll. 'If you want more money, just say so, but don't try any of your evil tricks on me.'

The witch fixed her evil eyes on him.

'You guessed the truth,' she said, 'it is only a little more money poor Pexie wants.'

Again the claw-like hand was held out. Black Coll would not touch it, but threw the money on the table.

'When shall I get the charm?' he asked.

'You must come back here in twelve days.'

Then, promising to come back at the agreed time, he went away.

In twelve days Black Coll got the promised charm. He sewed it into a cloth of gold, and put it on a fine chain. Then he put it into a box. It looked very pretty.

## An evil plan

Two weeks passed. How could Black Coll find the chance to put the charm around the neck of the Colonel's daughter? More money was dropped into Pexie's greedy hand, and then she agreed to help him.

One morning the witch dressed herself in better clothes. She combed her black hair, covered it with a snow-white cloth, and by magic, made herself look younger. Then she went out into the hills to gather mushrooms. Every morning, for two weeks, the cook at the Colonel's house bought mushrooms from her. Every morning she left a bunch of flowers for Miss Evleen Blake, saying that she had never seen her, but had heard that she was so pretty.

At last, one morning, she met Miss Evleen. She went up to her and gave her the flowers herself.

'Ah,' said Evleen, 'it is you who leave me flowers every morning. They are very sweet.'

'I pick them in the mountains. Has my lady ever been up into the big mountains?' asked Pexie.

'No,' replied Evleen, laughing. She was sure she could not walk up a mountain.

'Oh, but you should go,' said Pexie. 'Go with your friends, and ride on pretty little donkeys. There are many beautiful things for you to see up there.'

She told Evleen such wonderful stories about the mountains that Evleen began to think that she must go.

Not long after this Black Coll received a message

from Pexie. She told him that a group of people from the big house would go into the mountains the next day. Evleen Blake would be with them. Black Coll must be ready to feed a crowd of tired and hungry people, who in the evening would be brought to the Devil's Inn.

Black Coll was very busy. He managed, probably by black magic, to prepare a great feast for his expected guests. His empty rooms suddenly became full of beautiful furniture and pictures. Servants appeared from nowhere, and stood ready to carry in the wonderful food.

At last, the tired party came in sight of Black Coll's house, and Black Coll went out to ask them to come inside. Colonel Blake was very pleased to see him. Evleen had not told her father about Black Coll's strange behaviour towards her.

Everyone went into the feast except for Evleen Blake. She stayed outside. She was tired, but did not want to rest there. She was hungry, but she did not want to eat Black Coll's food. Black Coll and the Colonel came to the door and begged her to enter, the servants brought her food, but she would not go in, and she would not eat.

'Poison, poison,' she whispered, and threw the food away. But it was different when Pexie, the kindly old woman, the mushroom seller with all the wicked lines smoothed out of her face, came to the door. She brought a dish of cooked mushrooms to Evleen.

'Ah, my lady,' she said, 'I have cooked these just for you.' Then Evleen took the plate and ate all the mushrooms. She had hardly finished when she began to feel very sleepy, and she sat down on the door-step.
5   She put her head against the side of the door, and was soon fast asleep.

'Silly girl,' said the Colonel when he found her. He picked her up and carried her into one of the rooms. It had been empty that morning, but now contained a
10   beautiful bed. The Colonel laid his daughter on the bed and took his last look at her lovely face.

リューナイト  取

## The charm works

The Colonel went back to his friends, and soon after, the whole group went out to watch the beautiful sunset.
15   Black Coll went with them, but when they had gone some distance, he remembered he had to go back and fetch something. He was not away long, but he was away long enough to go into the room where Evleen was still sleeping and place a golden chain round her neck.
20   The Burrag-bos slipped among the folds of her dress.

After he had gone, Pexie crept to the door. She opened it a little, and sat down on a mat outside. An hour passed, and Evleen Blake still slept. After that she began to move, and Pexie knew she was waking up.
25   Soon, a sound in the room told her that the girl was awake and had got up. Pexie put her face to the open door and looked in. Evleen gave a scream of fear, and ran from the house.

It was nearly dark now, and the group was returning
30   towards the Devil's Inn. Some ladies, who were far in front of the others, met Evleen Blake. She came towards them and they noticed something bright, like gold, hanging round her neck. They went to talk to her, but

she stared at them in a strange way, and passed on. They thought she was very rude to behave like that.

Evleen ran on. A rabbit crossed her path and she laughed loudly. Clapping her hands she ran after it. Then she stopped and talked to the stones, hitting them with her hand when they did not answer her. Soon she began to call after the birds in a wild voice. Some of the gentlemen heard the noise and stopped to listen.

'What's that?' asked one.

'A young eagle,' said Black Coll, 'they often cry like that.'

'It was very much like a woman's voice,' said another. As he spoke another wild sound rang out from the rocks above. There was a piece of rock sticking out over a steep drop to the valley below. As they watched, they saw Evleen Blake moving towards this dangerous place.

'My Evleen,' cried the Colonel. 'She is mad to walk up there.'

'Mad,' repeated Black Coll, and he began to run as fast as his powerful legs would carry him.

When he came near her, Evleen had almost reached the very edge of the rock. He moved very carefully towards her, meaning to catch her in his arms before she knew he was there. Then he could carry her to safety. But at that moment Evleen turned her head and saw him. She gave a loud scream of hate and fear. A step back brought her within a foot of death.

Black Coll caught her, but one look into her eyes told him he was holding a mad woman. Back, back, she dragged him, and he had nothing to hold on to. The rock was slippery. Back, back she pulled him. There was a scream, a mad swinging backwards and forwards, and then the rock was empty against the sky. No one was there. Black Coll and Evleen Blake lay on the ground, together, far below.

# 7

# THE GOBLINS AND
# THE SEXTON

### Angry and miserable

In a small old English town, a long, long time ago, there
was a sexton called Gabriel Grub. He worked in the
church, and most of the work he did was done in the
churchyard, digging graves.

He was a lonely old man, and he was always angry.
He had only one friend, and that was himself. He
looked at every other merry face with a scowl of evil
temper, which, of course, frightened the people and
stopped them from trying to be friendly with him.

One Christmas Eve, a little before it got dark, Gabriel
put his spade on his shoulder, lit his lamp, and set off
for the churchyard. A grave had to be dug by next
morning, and as he was feeling unhappy,
he thought if he finished
the grave he would
feel much better.

As he walked through the town, he noticed the cheerful lights gleaming through the old windows, and heard the loud laughter and merry shouts of the people in the houses. He knew they were busy preparing for Christmas. He could see the clouds of steam rising from the pots, and smell the delicious food they were cooking. All this made Gabriel feel even more angry; and when groups of children ran out of the houses, laughing and playing their Christmas games, Gabriel scowled at them. He held the handle of his spade more tightly and walked on, thinking about horrible looking ghosts which would frighten the little boys and girls away.

These nasty thoughts made him feel much better. Soon he reached the lane near the churchyard. He liked this dark lane, because it was a nice, lonely place, and the people from the town never went there except when the sun was shining. Because of this, he was surprised and angry to hear somebody in the lane singing a jolly song about a merry Christmas.

As Gabriel walked on, and the voice came nearer, he saw it was a small boy who was singing. The boy was going to a party, and he was singing loudly to keep himself from feeling frightened in that lonely lane. So Gabriel waited until the boy came up to him, and then jumped on him, shouted at him, pushed him into a corner, and knocked him on the head with his lamp five or six times, to teach him to be quieter. The boy ran away with his hand to his head, singing quite a different sort of tune. Gabriel Grub laughed happily to himself, entered the churchyard, and locked the gate behind him.

He took off his coat, put down his lamp, and got into the unfinished grave. He worked for an hour or so quite cheerfully, even though the earth was hard and it was

not easy to break it and lift it out. There was a moon that night, but it did not give much light on the grave, which was in the shadow of the church. At any other time this would have made Gabriel angry and
5  miserable, but now he was very happy because he had stopped the boy singing.

## A most unusual creature

'Ho! Ho!' laughed Gabriel Grub, as he sat down on his favourite resting-place, which was a flat tombstone.
10  'Ho! Ho! Ho!' repeated a voice, just behind him.

Gabriel stopped laughing, and looked round. The churchyard was still and quiet in the pale moonlight. Snow lay hard and smooth upon the ground. Not one faint noise broke the silence of this lonely place. It
15  seemed as if sound itself was frozen.

'It was the echoes,' said Gabriel Grub.

'It was not,' said a deep voice.

Gabriel jumped up, and then stood very still with amazement and terror; for he saw something which
20  frightened him very, very much.

Close to him there was a most unusual creature sitting on an upright tombstone. His legs, which were extremely long, were crossed under him. His thin arms were bare, and his hands rested on his knees. On his
25  fat, round body he wore a short cloak, all covered with strange coloured designs; and the collar of this cloak was cut into curious points which stood up round his neck. His shoes curled up at his toes into long points also. On his head he had a hat which was wide at the
30  bottom and with a point at the top, and pinned to the hat was one large feather. This hat was covered with the white snow, and the goblin looked as if he had been sitting on the same tombstone, very comfortably,

for two or three hundred years. He was sitting perfectly
still; and he was smiling at Gabriel Grub with the kind
of unpleasant smile which only a goblin can make.

'It was not the echoes,' repeated the goblin.

Gabriel Grub was so frightened that he could not   5
speak.

'And what are you doing here on Christmas Eve?'
asked the goblin.

'I came to dig a grave, sir,' said Gabriel Grub.

'What sort of man wanders among graves and   10
churchyards on such a night as this?' cried the goblin.

'Gabriel Grub! Gabriel Grub!' screamed hundreds of
voices together. The sound seemed to fill the
churchyard. Gabriel looked round in terror, but he
could see nothing.   15

The goblin put out his tongue at the trembling Grub,
and then raising his voice, he said:

'And who, then, belongs to us?'

'Gabriel Grub! Gabriel
Grub!' shouted the   20
wild voices again.

The goblin smiled a
broader smile than before,
as he said 'Well, what do
you say about this?'   25

The grave-digger tried very hard to speak. 'It's — it's — very curious, sir,' he replied, half dead with fright, 'but I think I'll go back and finish my work, sir, if you don't mind.'

5 'Oh, the grave, eh?' said the goblin. 'Who digs graves on Christmas Eve when other men are merry — and who enjoys doing it?'

Again the mysterious voices shouted, 'Gabriel Grub! Gabriel Grub!'

10 'I'm sorry, but it seems my friends want you, Gabriel,' said the goblin, putting out his tongue again — and a most amazing tongue it was — 'Ah, yes, it seems my friends want you, Gabriel. We know the man with the angry face and the terrible look who came down 15 the street tonight, thinking bad thoughts about little children. We know the man who frightened and hit the boy, because he was jealous that the boy could be merry, and he could not. We know him, we know him.'

20 And then the goblin laughed a loud, high laugh, and threw his legs up in the air and stood on his head, or rather on the point of his tall hat. Then he rolled over and over, right to the grave-digger's feet, and there he sat with his legs crossed under him again. 'I — I must 25 leave you now, sir,' said the poor grave-digger, making an effort to move.

'Leave us!' cried the goblin. 'Gabriel Grub is going to leave us! Ho! Ho! Ho!'

## The goblins' cave

30 As the goblin laughed, hundreds of other goblins rushed into the churchyard, and began jumping backwards and forwards over the tombstones, without ever stopping to rest or take a breath.

The game became faster and faster as the goblins leaped faster and faster. They rolled and rolled all over the place, and flew like footballs all around the graves. The grave-digger's brain was beginning to go round and round as he watched the goblins; and then, suddenly, the goblin king jumped towards him, put his hand upon his collar, and sunk down with him into the earth.

They went down very fast. When Gabriel Grub had had time to get his breath, which had been taken away by the speed of his descent, he found that he was in what appeared to be a large cave. All round him were crowds of goblins, ugly and angry looking. Sitting on a raised seat in the middle of the room was his friend from the churchyard — the goblin king.

'It's cold tonight,' said the king of the goblins, 'very cold. Let's have a cup of something warm to drink!'

At this command, half a dozen goblins hastily disappeared, and presently returned with a cup of liquid fire. This they presented to the king.

'Ah!' cried the goblin, whose cheeks and throat shone as he swallowed the flames, 'this warms one, indeed! Bring another cup for Mr Grub!'

It was useless for the unhappy grave-digger to refuse it. One of the goblins held him while another poured the burning liquid down his throat. Then the whole crowd roared with laughter as he coughed and choked and wiped away the tears which poured from his eyes.

'And now,' said the king, 'show to this man of misery and anger a few of the pictures from our great collection.'

As the goblin king said this, a thick cloud, which hid the far end of the cave, slowly disappeared. Behind it there was a small room with cheap furniture, but everything was neat and clean. A group of little children were playing round their mother's chair.

Occasionally the mother rose and went to the window
to see if someone was coming. At last there was a knock
on the door; the mother opened it, and the children
crowded round her and clapped their hands as their
father entered. Then, as he sat down in his favourite
chair, they climbed over his knees, and his wife sat
beside him. All seemed to be happiness and comfort.

But then the scene began to change. Now there was
a small bedroom, and in it the youngest and most
beautiful child lay dying. Even as Gabriel watched him
with a feeling of interest which he had never felt before,
the child's brothers and sisters crowded round the little
bed and lifted his tiny hand, so cold and heavy. But
the touch of his cold hand frightened them, and in fear,
they looked at his little face; for they saw he was dead.

'What do you think of that?' said the goblin, turning
his large face towards Gabriel Grub.

Gabriel said something about it
being very sad, and he looked a little
ashamed as the goblin looked
at him with angry eyes.

'You miserable man!' said
the goblin, and he lifted up
his long thin legs and gave
Gabriel Grub a good hard
kick. Immediately after

this all the goblins started kicking him, without any mercy, just to teach him a good hard lesson.

'Show him some more!' said the king of the goblins.

## Gabriel learns at last

Many times the cloud came and went, and many lessons it taught to Gabriel Grub, who, although his back was very sore from the goblins' kicks, watched every scene with interest. He saw that men who worked hard were cheerful and happy; and he saw that even for people who had no education, the beauty of nature was a never-ending joy. He saw that men like himself, who scowled at the cheerfulness of others, were the most evil creatures in the world. And most important of all, when he compared all the good in the world with all the evil, he suddenly realized that this world was a very pleasant place after all.

As soon as he had realized this, the cloud which had just covered the last picture began to spread around him. One by one, the goblins faded from his sight; and as the last one disappeared, he fell asleep.

The day had dawned when Gabriel Grub woke up. He found that he was lying on the flat tombstone in the churchyard. His coat, spade, and lamp were scattered on the ground, and were all white with new snow. The stone on which he had first seen the goblin stood upright before him, and the grave which he had been digging the night before was not far away.

At first he began to wonder if his adventures had really happened, but he felt a great pain in his back when he tried to stand up, and then he knew he had indeed been kicked by the goblins. So he stood up as well as he could, and after he had brushed the snow off his coat, he put it on, and went back towards the town.

## What happened to the sexton?

But he had changed, and he could not bear to think of returning to a place where no one would either believe his story, or believe that he had changed. He hesitated
5  for a few seconds, and then set off to look for some other place where men would welcome him, and children would not run away from him in fear.

The lamp and the spade were found that day in the churchyard. At first everyone had their own opinion
10  about what had happened to the grave-digger, but some of the children decided that he had been carried away by the goblins. After a while this story was generally believed. In fact, after a few years, the people of that town began to think the story was actual history and
15  that is the way they think of it even today.

# QUESTIONS AND ACTIVITIES

## CHAPTER 1

*What happened in these places? Put the information in the right boxes.*

| Place | What happened |
|---|---|
| 1 **London** | (a) Blamyre delivers the letters and returns to his hotel with Lefebre. |
| 2 **Dover** | (b) The train breaks down and the luggage is put on another van. |
| 3 *on the boat from Dover* | (c) Blamyre receives a telegram telling him he is in danger. |
| 4 **Paris** | (d) Blamyre, Levison and the Baxters change trains for Marseilles. |
| 5 **Dromont** | (e) Levison tells Blamyre his combination lock words. |
| 6 *between Dromont and Fort Rouge* | (f) Blamyre meets Major Baxter and Levison in the passenger lounge. |
| 7 **Fort Rouge** | (g) Schwarzmoor tells Blamyre he must take two boxes of gold to Italy. |
| 8 *between Fort Rouge and Lyons* | (h) Major Baxter breaks Levison's bottle of champagne. |
| 9 **Lyons** | (i) A porter carrying one of the boxes nearly falls into the water. |
| 10 **Marseilles** | (l) The Major stops Blamyre shouting out his combination lock words. |

## CHAPTER 2

*Which of these sentences are true? Say what is wrong with the false ones.*

1   George Eade loved Susan Archer, the sister of a farmer.
2   Susan's parents thought Susan was not good enough for George.
3   Geoffrey Gibbs said he would give Susan a lot of money if she married him.
4   Susan went to stay with her aunt at Ormiston until the day of her wedding.
5   Soon afterwards, George learned that Susan had married Geoffrey Gibbs.
6   George's heart turned to gold, and he never spoke about Susan after that.

## CHAPTER 3

*Where should the second sentences (B) go so that they tell us more about the first sentences (A)? (The narrator is the person who tells the story.)*

| A | B |
|---|---|
| 1   After reading the news-paper, the narrator thought he saw the bedroom where the murder had happened. | (a)  Then he handed it to the narrator. |
| 2   He saw two men walking along the street. The first looked angry, the face of the second was the colour of grey wax. | (b)  But all the people he stood near felt very uncomfortable. |
| 3   In his bedroom he saw the second man beckoning to him. | (c)  The dead man stood by each man's bed. |
| 4   In the room where the jurymen slept, he saw the figure of the dead man. | (d)  No one else seemed to see them. |

5 When a picture of the dead man was shown in court, the figure snatched the picture.

(e) There was no dead body on the bed.

6 No one except the narrator could see the dead man in the court room.

(f) Then the figure was gone.

7 After the jury decided the prisoner was guilty, the figure shook a grey cloth over itself.

(g) He said the narrator had put a rope round his neck.

8 The prisoner said that he had seen the narrator before.

(h) The narrator's servant suddenly knew what he had seen.

## CHAPTER 4

*The underlined sentences are in the wrong paragraphs. Write them out in the right place.*

1 A year ago the signalman saw the strange figure standing by the red light near the tunnel. The figure seemed to be able to make the telegraph bell ring. Six hours later a terrible accident happened.

2 Six months afterwards he saw the figure by the red light again. The signalman ran to it, but when he pulled at its sleeve, the figure disappeared. That same day, a beautiful young lady died suddenly in the train.

3 A week ago the figure had appeared once more, waving and calling out. It was leaning against the post and had both its hands in front of its face. The signalman was worried because he did not know what the figure was warning him about.

## CHAPTER 5

*Choose the right words to say what this part of the story is about.*

The Baron began to think that nothing was so (1) **good/bad** that it could not be made better. An empty purse might one day be filled again. Scolding (2) **wives/sisters** could be quietened. Twelve children could not all go (3) **well/wrong**. The ghost got angry. It thought that the Baron was (4) **joking/crying**. It wanted the Baron to hurry up and leave this (5) **terrible/ wonderful** life at once.

Then the Baron thought he might not be any (6) **better/worse** off when he had left this world. He decided that he would (7) **stop/start** feeling sorry for himself. He would go and (8) **shout at/speak to** the Baroness. He would try hunting bears again. Then he (9) **fell back into/jumped up on** his chair, laughing. The ghost gave a (10) **quiet/terrible** scream and disappeared.

## CHAPTER 6 (A)

*Put the words at the end of each sentence in the right order.*

1  Black Coll loved Evleen Blake, but   [of] [she] [afraid] [him] [was].
2  One day Black Coll heard a woman   [Burrag-bos] [talking] [about] [the].
3  Tying it round someone's neck, would   [that] [love] [you] [make] [person].
4  There was an old woman called Pexie   [the] [make] [could] [Burrag-bos] [who].
5  Black Coll gave Pexie some money   [to] [Burrag-bos] [get] [the] [him] [for].
6  He gave her some more money to help him   [round] [put] [neck] [it] [Evleen's].

## CHAPTER 6 (B)

*Put these sentences in the right order to say what this part of the story is about. Start with sentence number 3.*

1  She climbed to the top of a steep rock and stood near the edge.
2  There, Pexie gave Evleen a dish of mushrooms to eat.
3  Pexie met Evleen and told her many stories about the mountains.

4  The Burrag-bos made Evleen go mad.

5  There was a scream and then they were both lying dead on the ground below.

6  When they were in the mountains they came to Black Coll's house.

7  When she was asleep Black Coll placed the Burrag-bos round her neck.

8  Black Coll ran to save her, but she dragged him back with her.

9  Evleen decided to go to the mountains with her father and her friends.

10  The mushrooms made Evleen fall asleep.

## CHAPTER 7

*Put the letters of these words in the right order.*

Gabriel Grub was a (1) **nyolle**, angry old man. He looked at every merry face with a scowl of evil (2) **pemtre**. He was angry when people were being merry at Christmas time. He did not like to hear their loud (3) **trughale** and merry shouts. He frightened a small boy who was (4) **nigsign** a jolly Christmas song. Gabriel Grubb (5) **donkeck** the boy on the head with his lamp.

The goblins thought Gabriel Grub (6) **obdeglen** to them. They took him down into their cave. They poured a burning (7) **quildi** down his throat. Behind a cloud of smoke at the far end of the cave they showed him (8) **stricupe** of people who had worse lives than him. Then they kicked him without (9) **rymce** to give him a good hard lesson. After this Gabriel (10) **azderile** that this world was a very pleasant place after all.

Oxford
Progressive
English Readers